CHASERS

✿

CHASERS

✳

STEPHEN IRA

NEW MICHIGAN PRESS
TUCSON, ARIZONA

NEW MICHIGAN PRESS

DEPT OF ENGLISH, P. O. BOX 210067

UNIVERSITY OF ARIZONA

TUCSON, AZ 85721-0067

<http://newmichiganpress.com>

Orders and queries to <nmp@thediagram.com>.

ISBN 978-1-934832-88-2. FIRST PRINTING.

Design by Ander Monson.

Cover image by Chris Berntsen.

CONTENTS

for Chris

Why sometimes, when I'm talking
    do I suddenly have nothing to say? Why
do I hold you in my arms
    in certain dreams, certain nights, and in others
chase you endlessly across
    the Fields of Mars, into the swirling Tiber?

—Horace, Ode IV.i, trans. Richard Howard

The cis people were frightened; they seemed to have appeared so
    suddenly.
The cis people reeled and their robes spun out over the earth.
On land there were still outposts. There were encampments.
The cis people were sad. They "gnashed" their "teeth."
In winter, in the snow, looking out at it, they were quietly moved.
The cis people lay awake naming names they had known.
The cis people decided to begin by touching one of each: dog, pig,
    horse.
On the lake there were houseboats. In the beach towns, gold.
The cis people were rejected at the gender clinic and learned.
The cis people heard their own names and so committed arson.
    Prosaic decision.
There were no cis people. Considered intersectionally, the theory did
    not make sense.
The cis people had beautiful dances, slow, melancholy, with tall
    spindly puppets.
The cis people cooked cabbage, chewed at night, prescribed numbers
    of times;
they were "religious." They were "in grief." "Gnashing"
their "teeth." The cis people had things to say but fell silent.
In the city, at the building and loan, in the ski lodge.
The cis people, in their palatial homes, had big old faces like raw marble,
as hard to climb as the curved sky, the one our ancestors knew,
that was spotted yet somehow featureless, and feared.
When the moon rang and rang up there, I knew I could feel them.

NO ECHO

I thought it was that you got off
on talk about cum, but then
you're stretching me out
with my spot in your hand
and it comes to me, clear
and slick—I see, it's
because I said I wished
I could shoot. I said so
a few times. It's true—
I only know how much so
once I say it. Most of the time
cis people just walk around,
fucking everyone with their huge stuff
and either cannot or choose not
to see the dark liquid
that makes cave noise
between the body and an
answer to its question.
Another body, everyone
has that, a moonlike body
in another world.
Most of the time living people just
walk around, pretending
only transsexuals have them,
because we're better at it
and for much worse reasons.

But could you ever
have another body? God,
I hope not. I remember
thinking, I can't forget
the freckles resting
on his shoulders,
like an avant garde scarf,
the second time. No echo
in the cave. What could
improve? But I'm sure,
in there, you reach its end
somehow, dodging cars
on a bike, some arduous
activity like that. How hot.
The shady beach with still pools
and the overhang. The afternoon
dark from some quirk
of the land and the sun.
The water dark and cool and a relief
to my God-given hot body,
shaking while you say,
"I wanna bathe in your cum."
Why does anything I say sound
like I don't like it? I like it.

JACOB RIIS MEMORIAL BEACH

Two good poems in a three day fuck
is a decent ratio, so I'm not trying
to go too hard here, but I thought
I'd be stupid to so to speak "waste"
a day at the beach. Lots to talk
about with water, and the cops
and my nerves and your friends. I walked
a lot around a little patch of sand.
I almost don't want to say anything,
but it feels so good. I keep going
and everything keeps walking around
interrupting me, including you—not
in like, a bad way, just like how
Chartreuse showed up on the corner,
or the woman walking the gay beach
calling how she's selling rum punch,
or you trying to pick my stuck door
with my lace needles, or me writing
in the middle of the night because
I'm too turned on to sleep because
you kiss in your sleep, and you're
sleeping—or anything like that,
like, anything suddenly there.

Hello Chris. I told you once—with a poem,
I can talk to anyone I want, no matter what
I'm talking about. That's why I like them.
I can talk to just anyone.—Then I wrote poems
to you, about you, over and over, far from you,
one after the other. I couldn't stop carrying them.
Like the colorless voice mouthing my thoughts
inside me found a housemate. A new friend
who speaks only of you. A second self
with room in his life for all this love.
Who talks only about you, and only to you,
and only when you're somewhere else.
We came to tell you—Transsexuality frightens
us, it confesses how much beauty matters
to life.—I couldn't say this to just anybody,
or even you, if you were here. I couldn't say—
I'm shocked you want to touch me—
when you touched me. We weren't in a
poem. The only place you are now
is my voice. I love that. When I saw
you last, you had some heavy questions
about suffering and God, and I was like,
being trans is how I know He visited
and found the body mattered. It was truthful,
changeable, worth enough to change
but not to plan on, not forever,
but Chris, I couldn't say that.

BELLS, HILLS

I ran around all summer,
and it came on September

before I knew to stop pretending
it was summer still.

Would I have settled for red leaves,
experienced the end of feminine

hysteria in Iowa? Perhaps,
if my feelings weren't moving

so fast they were masking your absence.
So back to the flyover country I flew,

in a fit of deep pique, provoked by
what wasn't enough—not you, not what

you felt, but something else.
Well, once I went away from you

not even you were waiting there.
I'm lonely here. Two men in my whole town

remind me of my life, plus Liam,
of course, & Kevin and Mark—maybe Will,

Nicki Minaj's lab partner in high school
in New York. "Wow! Any stories?" "No

stories. She's a nice girl." I've never even met
the men I mention: one wheels

his lover in his chair, the other wears
a wide-brimmed hat, jewels pinned

all over it. Most of the grown
townies I know around don't trust them.

I'd like to introduce you, when you come,
but as I said, we've never met. And what

reminds me of me makes me angry,
anyway, I love you daddy, please be safe.

NO SNOW

I woke up without you,
wondering where…? and there
was all that snow, enclosing
rounding softening
everything, and clean.
I wanted to lie there until you came back,
and that's what I want now, but I'm here
and you've never been here.
They said snow might
come in today but no, I guess
it's bored, opted to skip us.
I'm sorry to hear it's cruel there,
where it's warm. Here is snowless,
sweet, and boring cold.
Liam has a date at the glory hole
today; I thrash alone in our sheets
and literally say—out loud!—
when I come, your name.
I had hoped it would snow. I would
wake and look from my bed
and I'd see it touch everything
as precisely as you touch
my body and the rest
of me. And I'd think, he has risen early,
to work, but will be back,
and roll over and sleep and wait.

LOVE LINE

When I was very young,
before I knew what
I was or that you
loved it, or who
you were, or whether
I would spend
my life alone—so,
very young, the nanny
and I listened to Love Line
on the night drive
to elocution class.
And one night someone,
some guy, called in
about trans women,
which wasn't the term
he used or one
I knew. He wanted
to fuck one. It was
all he wanted, all
that he thought of—
he could not fuck
without the thought,
"You know what might
feel better…"
and the doctor
said: hire a hooker

get this out of your system
you can't have a relationship
with a person like that,
which was in a way true,
a way specific to
that caller's hunger—
not how the doctor
thought of it at all.
I sat where a poised
young woman did not
sit, and thought
I would hate
Dr. Drew as long as I
could stay alive.
I don't recall connecting
any of this to anything,
not my anger,
not treating death
like a bad super
when I had never wanted
for a thing in life.
"*Please* fix those pipes."
I used to love to
hear the troubles
grown up people
had with the game
they'd invented—did
they do it just

to hate it? I never
doubted I would out-
perform them. Funny,
huh? I have always
identified as good
at head, before I ever
gave it, like how
I knew I'd like you
in advance of speaking
to you, like how you knew
when you saw
the first you saw
(God rest her soul), that life
would take a turn now,
and you'd spend it
driving us to appointments,
wiping up vomit,
helping us move.

Get in the car: poop-poop! You freak out about your dick, I'm well-equipped. Everyone panics her dick, clockwork. This one is a very rare clock. You cry on the beach: "I should have been a butch." "You should, but you would have transitioned." (Keening): "Oh!" (Same figure, not keening): "I know." I find boys to put your fist inside—we wake up to gossips sipping their nitrous nearby. His name is NOT Oliver but in his overalls he's guilty that he made you sad. Now you're sprawled wheelbarrow-ward with me. All men are only halfway here, even when we're alone. What will be your next fanaticism? This time, we'll make it one I share.

I got all choked up and I threw down my gun
and said, "Worship me. I need to be worshipped
and you're one of the ones who will worship me.
You're combing this country all night," I said,
"the river and the barns, the houses where the stingy
hand out potatoes to my sisters—*Leaning,
leaning, safe and secure from all alarms*—
with LOVE on one hand and HATE on the other,
searching out somebody like me to worship.
To worship what won't name itself! I hate to say
what I am, how I hate it! All "terms" make me feel
like a child, a doctor, or a child doctor, Doogie
Howser, Freddie Highmore, I hate it, I hate it!
You listen," I said, "I said, 'Worship me!
Take a knee, take two, take as many as you
need, take my knees, take my picture,
I didn't know I had it before your camera
pressed against my crotch, please take it,
please take it away. I mean too much. I'm not
an end,'" I said, I said, "Please, come here, I'm hard
for little things, and if we ever have a son,
I promise to name him whatever I am."

ROOM

All the time! I try to conceive of us,
not planning but settled, and close—
say, within groping distance. I'm trans,
I can't walk across rooms. I'm trans,
all the houses I've lived in have numberless
rooms. Someone told me once, one of my teachers,
that I said I too much. I made sentences.
I started them each time with I. Chris,
I try all the time. I imagine worlds
with us in them but in all those worlds,
I'm thinking; I'm alone. No one else presses
the stalk of their thought on my thought. Chris,
come wherever I am right now—I can't see the walls,
I cannot feel the molding on the ornate doors.

LITTLE PLANK

In this manicured room built by working class boyfriends, if I keep my clothes on, I look just like James Merrill. Right hand on my father's checkbook and the left on my planchette. Left hand on a letter from Elizabeth. It describes animals she saw have gender, not money, not unmoney. Right hand in my cunt, pulling on wires, refining, affirming the form. Voices of dead people under my hand. It's a scam, and they move when I move.

DYSSOMNIAS

You said, it's
all right, it's still
early, you can sleep
a little longer,
and climbed back
into bed to hold
me and to pet my hair.
My hair. But
loving you is not
a good feeling.
My bitter skin,
winning or losing
battle. You might
ask why. Did I—I
do not know. My
ribs? My stomach?
Possibly. If so,
then no, I don't
remember that. Below
my hip is all right,
though. I did say,
actually—you forgot,
in part maybe because
you have a stark
emotional CV. It knows
what severity is:

what men remember
and what no one
would forgive.
Struggling as you kiss
my ribs, two minutes.
Two minutes forgiving
you, two, three. Sorry
about no moaning
and the straw over
the garden—it was like
education: I wanted
to like it. Two seconds, you
agree, repeat,
when I say it
was not that
bad, what happened
with my body
and the others. You
refused to fight me,
it made me so
mad, it was funny.
I would lie safe
on his warm chest
like a drowned body on the lip
of some strange country.
That was before it
started—sometimes I was
frightened, but at that point

it was not that bad.
On second thought,
I wouldn't know when
it began, or if it ended
ever. Let me lie there
again, in your bed,
and sleep longer
with you nearer
despite how what was
not that bad
has made loving,
loving anyone, loving
you, not a good feeling.

> Why is it you always get to sit in the shade
> While I have to stand in the sun?
> —Dot, *Sunday in the Park with George*

I have always struggled with
not being loved enough
to preclude all possible pain
for my lover, which is insane,
and you have always struggled
with being impossible. I know
now. Apparently. Once—
you were lovely, I wasn't sure why
but I thought of you constantly—
Twice—you folded all my towels,
couldn't be real, I posted:
"I throw a glass of beet juice
at the wall." Three times—
for days I was deliriously
happy and then you were not real,
you disappeared, came back from work
and slept and then could only sleep,
complain, and say I couldn't help.
How long you've been a man!
It makes me feel like Nathan Lane,
or Jessica Waters as Lucille Bluth,
or Bernadette Peters as Dot,

waiting for you to stop painting
except you're not painting—taking
pictures, rather—if you were
you'd be much happier. I like
when they're of me. Damned
and cursed before all the world,
that is what I want to be.

LITTLE BIRD

I sang all night for you, but you didn't care. You were too sad. *Little bird*, I said to myself, *you can't bring anybody back, but maybe you can keep him here.* I thought you liked my song. But I couldn't tell now. You looked angry, but you stayed in the room where I sang. I inherited the song. Not from my parents. Not from my grandmother. My grandfather doesn't sing. My song was mine and I thought you liked it. I thought you loved me. Now you showed no sign of loving anything. But you stayed in the room all night. The room was full of statues with coins under their tongues. I felt bad for building them. Some don't even have names. Sylvia, Ian, Sam, Emily, Ann. You barely moved. Sometimes, you moved. *Little bird*, I told myself, *little bird*, pretending I was you, *I love you. Please sing for me.* I didn't want you to leave. I kept singing.

POEM

I loved him so much
my heart flew out
of all frameworks for power
I knew, and I thought
he was different and I
waited to find out
what that meant, but given
time, discovered
he's not different, they're just not
all the same, and that
was terrifying, terrifying news.

> There's nane that gaes by Carterhaugh
> But they leave him a wad,
> Either their rings, or green mantles,
> Or else their maidenhead.
> —"Tam Lin," version 39A,
> *The English and Popular Ballads* 1882-1898

I.

I had been warned, of course, many times. I found the grounds of the ruin. I pinged you by breaking the stem on this rose, most versions suggest. I can't believe how long we used condoms! All those warnings! But the world of men said I was sterile. We knew better. Let me say it again, the same way: without you behind the bar, would I still love the kingdom fairy ointment let me see? Small dust of leather earth that walks so arrogantly— Pregnant, I brim with ointment of my own. I try to find the fairies. Who needs theory with conspiracies like these? Which ones I respect, which depress me. Which speak only French to you, out of defensive affection. Which hold you prisoner, which hold you here. And then which attend you, excuse me. Which ones are a tithe, and then which ones are not.

2.

Before he got a baby on me, was I going to go back? One knight asks her who the father is. Nobody you know! she says. My lover rides a steed that's swifter than the wind. My love well-shod in hydrated and living second skin. My lover's past is murky, though we see him every day. Perhaps too much at Carterhaugh, perhaps too long away. He wears one glove, breaks uniform, or doesn't show at all—or he comes back in his full kit, and canvasses the wall. He kisses me when I come in, and hard-won faces change— but I hold tight and fear him not, and we leave for a bar with a stage.

UPSTAIRS AT THE PHOENIX I SAT DOWN AND WEPT

> The raunchiest, hands down, of the gay bars in town.
> The upstairs is something out of Dennis Cooper. If
> you don't know who he is, don't bother going up.
> —Brian S., *Yelp*

For me the whole production
seems to or does determine

whether I'm real, so I play hard.
I end up under barstools

pleased with the protein
full in my face,

watching the red rim
of the bar, working alone.

The LEDs uniquely
bright to me, from this angle,

down here by the boots. She's my
illumination. She may not

endure for long.

My pussy as thick as my tongue.
Just as wrong.

Wasn't it you, in the half light of the alders, who told me to follow and said not to be afraid? And wasn't I not? Wasn't that you, who seemed to know my face across that long expanse of—what, world? Didn't you dress in brass and battered copper, with eyes like the sky in a basin, and wake me so gently you frightened yourself? And weren't your eyes blue, but lighter than mine? Didn't you lift me with your good arms, up onto several beautiful things the people had built and abandoned? Weren't you the eagle who found me and said, "Now you're found," who handed me his cup to carry? Then I lived on the mountain with you and your sisters, my youth like a flag on your beauty, and we had such a view of the world. And wasn't it as if, up there, we could look down at the world and feel the dream coming off it? It was not like the world—because this dream was made for us. Chris, the world has a dream of itself that I touch when I'm with you. Weren't you the one, Chris, in the alders, who promised the world would forgive me for these little wounds, my feet? If you could remember that the world is where I found you, I would let it eat my heart. If I could remember that the world is where you found me, then I would never have to eat again.

THE CAKE DREAM

I.

In the dream this time, I made you a cake; so, in this dream, I was the kind of man who fluently makes cake for someone he loves, and you were who you really are: a man who wants some cake. One side of our little kitchen fell open—we lived on the side of a mountain. This delighted us every time. In the dream, I get on my knees while you eat. You put two fingers on my cheek, so I look up. "Baby," you say, "You know that if you're in control of it, it's not a dream, right? That's desire, or a fantasy." You are right. But it makes me mad. Still, other versions of the dream feature houses deep in the woods, and a child, and of these, which I sleep through, I am not in control.

2.

I lied again. The dream about our son—I made it up to tell you how I felt. Since then, I lost authorship of my lie, and I dream of our son like a "hidden reality," or an uncontrollable fact. Can't make anyone know it but me. That's why I beg to get bred. Sometimes, I wonder whether I can have children, but it's never a matter of "still." Besides, those are questions, not dreams.

3.

Once, in the dream, it was you, but with mirrored tattoos. The address of your old house on the right hand instead of the left. The broken clock fucked up by a scar on your left arm instead of the right. The rest of them. I knew either this wasn't you, or was an ancient somehow truer deeply evil part of you. With dread I realized: this might live inside all people, but from you I summoned it. Would it mewl when I had to kill it. What need we fear who knows it, when none can call our power to account? Neither is this a real sleep dream I had, but an unused idea for a story.

4.

I dreamed someone finally noticed that I kept my middle name. I got to tell about my book and Elizabeth Bishop. Mike says, everyone you meet in a dream you've met—exactly the pseudo-fact a poet loves. How do you check on that? Canvass your dreams for strangers? This person was strange to me, or I would have remembered them. When I explained that Elizabeth was the only part of my given name unfreighted with familial significance, they really got it, and just how that related to the arbitrary subjectivity Bishop swirls around "In the Waiting Room." They asked how my manuscript handled that poem's racism, because, they said, it sounded like too good of an idea to risk going badly, and that led to talk about how I could, and had to, tell the truth. If no one in dreams is a stranger, why couldn't that person be you?

5.

But the dream about you is different. It extends out into sleep, but is not limited to it. The dream about you has to do with politics, but not the way we feel them here and now. Your campaign does not, say, in the dream, reach viability in most of Iowa, so that I know I'll have a job until New Hampshire, in the dream. In other words, in these dreams about you I know the difference between wanting to do good and doing it; if I don't, I can adjust the fantasy. Often, when I sleep through dreams I know everything, say, about my manuscript, but of course can't carry it. Genet once asked a man if he were gay. The man confessed, for the first time, to any living soul, that he had had homosexual experiences. "Experiences?!" cried Genet. "Oh, no! I mean dreams, desires, fantasies!" Temporary knowledge is the best part of dreams.

6.

I dreamed I could fly. I fought my exgirlfriend, mischeviously. You asked, "Did you get angry at anyone today?" You were so mild. When I said no I figured you would know it was a lie, because the cops were listening. Hump on his back with three sticks coming out, but then the camera moved and pronoun changed from him to you. This is always happening once I nod off. The hunch began to fall; I saw it was a sweet potato, which accounted for the curve. He was worried about it at airport security.

7.

I always tell people this one. I've told you. During dinner, I had something in my bag that I wanted to show Alfred Hitchcock. But beneath all the copies of *The Normal Heart*, I couldn't find it. I just kept pulling copies out, and some playbills for it. Like, fifteen copies of *The Normal Heart*. Certainly didn't put them in my bag.

8.

In the dream, your gold skin feels gold. So does mine. In the dream, the horizon is frank, and at last it arrives with the deeds. These deeds have enough houses to hold all the boys in our lives, but still let us get married! Then, once we think twice, they're to everyone's houses, and we rip them up. They're a big neon sign reading: EVERYONE EATS. The first time I saw you as a figure in my fantasy, you were up in the barn, just swinging your legs like Huck Finn. I was ten feet below you in the parking lot. You were tinkering with the neon sign you'd made from scraps, and it said the name of that place.

9.

Bronco says that fantasies are more abstract than desires, and knowing this changed his whole life. Freud says that in a fantasy the "I" is mobile and can see itself. Howard Stern says, everyone should do psychotherapy. And I say, in the dream I can't tell the difference between you, me, and our son, who could be anyone.

10.

I remember now, as if I really dreamed it, the house in the woods, and the boy with his long blond hair, like crepe paper. You'd play in your workshop. I guess I'd have the name "Stephen." I don't know what it will be like. I do not sleep well, and it's rarely I remember what has happened there; the dream of the normal heart, for example, was long before we met, when I would write dreams down. I can't remember what we do in my mind without our consent. I wonder how different it is, in the dream.

I described you to McKenzie as my loved one. Don't see why I'd slow down for my heart. When I waited for so long to speak! I did, right before I came here. For you, I wrote poems that everyone loved, except those who resent my success, and wore a cream called skin food. The more you grieved for nothing, the more I sang to you. And then the more refined the people got who heard my little trill. I was scared of the other trans poets finding out that I'd fallen in love. I, my own loyalty. I, who grew up too young and alone for allegiance. Resolved: *I'll make my poem such that the man I love can't leave its lines. I'll name his difference from me like a hiss.* I, my persuasion, confused, saying to all your kind, "Be brought to my side! I, poet-self, transfigured into tiny icon, peering from my open mouth, I'll take your body in my lips and with it tell the truth." I, my. My disavowal different; I went to work on it, I know—so weatheréd I am, so pixie-faced, structuring courtly love so long from its outside. I insist. I, my, I, essentialist typewriter burning so that I cannot touch you, little Lord surviving his own will's rainbow—dense and unlikable to myself as cake. Could've solved this whole problem through getting less interesting. I wrote to you. I want Hollywood. I, my won't leave behind lyric problems. I, my realisms—pulling off "experimental" for so long without pulling my weight. The thing is, I remember even up until 2012 or so, it seemed really experimental for transsexuals to write lyric poetry. I have loved you. I have taken advantage of this.

LOVING YOU FOREVER ON THE MOON & IN THIS LIFE

As I lie next to you
tonight, I feel myself
vibrating quickly—
quickly enough
I could radiate up
to the moon.
I am so horny,
I've become imbued
with a white light,
but it's fine—fine,
it's fine! that you felt
too weird, after your awful
day at the doctor, fine,
we won't have sex. I lie
beside you staring at
your face, and it seems
bigger than my body,
it looks
      like a large scale
topographical map:
familiar shapes
in grays and blacks,
overlaid sometimes
with tiny transparent
dark blue or purple ovals,
like an old vhs tape.

The effect of staring
at a face too close
to see. So you get
that the white light
felt nice, then, right?
She really thought
she'd pour in. Were you
really lit by the moon?
Moon!—love's truest
tattered carry!
I lift her in my pussy,
like a man. The white light
put me in my body.
I remembered Christ—
claims I made, years
ago, in a poem to you,
about Christ.
   Do I believe?
I said there was one place.
I'm beside you tonight.
Beside you tonight, I am heavy
as if the light has lined my body
with the soil of the moon,
and you lie beside me,
transmitting: *Beauty matters*
to life.
   I'm lying prone
inside your memorized

beloved face, praising,
persuading you, the cis
man with the camera,
as love poems demand—
controlling you, as all
poems offer. I mastered
this practice. I lie next to you.
      We don't have sex.
No panic. I'm white light,
waves and floods. Lover, tranny
catcher, shutterbug,
you're here for good.
What will I write
without this rhetoric
to fill my hands?
I watch your face
in black and gray,
the ovals like old
video, my hips
and pussy thick
with soil from the moon.
I'm in a place called
"Loving You Forever
On the Moon
& In This Life."
         Tonight
the hairy moon
falls open in two halves

below your belly
to let me lick out light.
Your clit, an image.
You came, and you
flooded my poem.

ACKNOWLEDGMENTS

My thanks to the following publications, which published some of this work, some of it in slightly different forms: *DIAGRAM, Fence, No Tokens, DREGINALD, Paintbucket, Protean, Poetry (Chicago), Guesthouse, Ignota,* and the *Denver Quarterly.*

Special thanks to Chris Berntsen, Liam O'Brien, Kay Gabriel, Lee Carroll, Hal Schrieve, Maxe Crandall, Diana Cage, Nora Claire Miller, Bianca Messinger, Kamden Hilliard, Toby Altman, Jack Jung, Jules Wood, TJ, CJ, the Orleans Phoenix, Alicia Wright, Tracie Morris, Elizabeth Willis, DA Powell, David Groff, merritt kopas, Jane Huffman, and Katie Jean Shinkle. It takes help from so many people to talk about love.

STEPHEN IRA is a writer, filmmaker, and performer. He lives in New York. Publications include the *Poetry Project Newsletter*, *Poetry (Chicago)*, *DIAGRAM*, *Fence*, the *American Poetry Review*, *baest*, and *tagvverk*. In 2013, he was a Lambda Literary Fellow. In 2019, he completed an MFA at the Iowa Writers' Workshop. Favorite performance and filmmaking appearances include Sundance, OutFest, NewFest, and La Mama Etc.

※

COLOPHON

Text is set in a digital version of Jenson, designed by Robert Slimbach in 1996, and based on the work of punchcutter, printer, and publisher Nicolas Jenson. The titles here are also in Jenson.

❈

NEW MICHIGAN PRESS, based in Tucson, Arizona, prints poetry and prose chapbooks, especially work that transcends traditional genre. Together with DIAGRAM, NMP sponsors a yearly chapbook competition.

DIAGRAM, a journal of text, art, and schematic, is published bimonthly at THEDIAGRAM.COM. Periodic print anthologies are available from the New Michigan Press at NEWMICHIGANPRESS.COM.

CPSIA information can be obtained
at www.ICGtesting.com
Printed in the USA
BVHW042157041022
648707BV00004B/77

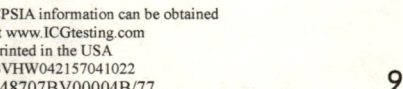

9 781934 832882